Tales from the Cryptocurrency

Tales from the Cryptocurrency

Rowan Everhart

CONTENTS

- Introduction — 1
- 1 The Rise of Cryptocurrencies — 3
- 2 Understanding Blockchain Technology — 6
- 3 Benefits and Risks of Cryptocurrencies — 9
- 4 Cryptocurrency Trading and Investment Strategies — 11
- 5 Regulatory Challenges in the Cryptocurrency Market — 13
- 6 Cryptocurrency and Financial Inclusion — 15
- 7 Cryptocurrency's Impact on Traditional Banking — 17
- 8 The Future of Cryptocurrencies — 20
- 9 Case Studies: Cryptocurrency Success Stories — 22
- 10 Cryptocurrency and Cybersecurity — 24

11 Cryptocurrency and Money Laundering 26

12 Cryptocurrency and Taxation 29

13 Cryptocurrency and International Remittances 32

14 Cryptocurrency and Decentralized Finance (DeFi) 35

Conclusion 38

Enjoyed This Book? Let Others Know! 40

Copyright © 2025 by Rowan Everhart
All rights reserved. No part of this book may be reproduced in any manner whatsoever without written permission except in the case of brief quotations embodied in critical articles and reviews.
First Printing, 2025

Introduction

In recent years, the rise of digital currencies has redefined the very concept of money, challenging traditional financial systems and reshaping global economic landscapes. This book seeks to provide a comprehensive exploration of cryptocurrency, beginning with the development of a cryptocurrency taxonomy that encompasses related parameters and tangible examples. Utilizing tools like Tableau and D3.js, we've created an interactive digital framework. This allows users to visualize critical data points such as type, number, market value, rarity, use case, and the consensus mechanisms employed in the digital currency ecosystem.

This exploration also examines the political ramifications of a cashless society, analyzing how digital currencies have been portrayed in ten major international newspapers. To achieve this, an automated data collection program was deployed, gathering 946 articles published between 2010 and 2018 in outlets including The New York Times, The Washington Post, The Guardian, Le Monde, Die Tageszeitung, and The China Post. Through joint content analysis, we explored key narratives around cryptocurrency, focusing on negative reports, blockade warnings, and business perspectives. By combining these insights with our taxonomy, we evaluate how the perceptions of blockchain and digital currencies evolve in the broader sociopolitical context. Our initial findings offer valuable groundwork for future research and similar studies.

Over the last decade, digital currencies have transformed access to money, particularly in regions without centralized banking systems. This decentralization, coupled with robust security measures and significant investment opportunities, has contributed to the proliferation of digital money, even in wealthier nations. Yet, despite its global momentum, skepticism persists across the political spectrum. Critics on the left voice concerns about the potential marginalization of low-income individuals and dissidents in a cashless society, fearing that financial systems could exclude or penalize them. On the right, some worry about the prospect of governments exploiting cashless systems to monitor or control citizens for political purposes.

The study of digital currencies has evolved into an interdisciplinary discourse, merging technology with politics. This book takes a balanced approach to analyze these dynamics, engaging with a diverse subset of stakeholders in the cryptocurrency world. By doing so, we aim to illuminate the multifaceted impact of digital currencies on society and contribute meaningfully to this increasingly crucial conversation.

1

The Rise of Cryptocurrencies

The story of modern cryptocurrency begins with a groundbreaking white paper published by an enigmatic figure known as Satoshi Nakamoto. This nine-page document, titled *Bitcoin: A Peer-to-Peer Electronic Cash System*, laid the foundation for a transformative digital currency system. Using simple language complemented by bullet points and diagrams, Nakamoto's white paper made an otherwise complex topic accessible to a wide audience. The concept was revolutionary yet straightforward—a system designed to function as seamlessly as cash exchanged in person. Nakamoto eloquently summarized the vision:

"What is needed is an electronic payment system based on cryptographic proof instead of trust, allowing any two willing parties to transact directly with each other without the need for a trusted third party."

This idea wasn't entirely new. The challenge of creating secure digital money had been discussed for years in technological circles, with one particularly persistent obstacle standing in the way: the double-spending problem. This problem, inherent to digital assets, arises when the same currency unit is spent more than once due to the absence of a centralized system to verify transactions. Nakamoto didn't invent the concept of digital currency; instead, he delivered an elegant solution—a decentralized method to prevent double-spending.

Nakamoto's innovative approach employed blockchain technology, a distributed ledger system that records transactions in a secure and immutable manner. Each transaction is verified by network participants through consensus mechanisms, eliminating the need for a central authority. This system not only solved the double-spending problem but also introduced an unprecedented level of transparency and security to digital transactions.

The implementation of this solution took time and refinement. On January 3, 2009, Bitcoin was officially launched as an open-source project, marking the birth of a new era in financial systems. It was designed as a peer-to-peer electronic cash system, enabling direct transactions between parties without the involvement of intermediaries, such as banks or payment processors. This decentralized nature made Bitcoin not just a currency but a movement—a challenge to traditional financial structures.

Dubbed the "missing piece of cyber currency" in 2008, Nakamoto's creation generated both curiosity and intrigue. Despite its monumental impact, Nakamoto's true identity remains one of the greatest mysteries of the digital age. The name "Satoshi Nakamoto" could belong to an individual or a group, but no concrete clues have emerged to uncover their identity. Like the anonymous authors of groundbreaking studies in Osaka, Japan, during the late 1970s, Nakamoto's anonymity has only added to the mystique surrounding Bitcoin's origin story.

The rise of Bitcoin laid the groundwork for an entire ecosystem of cryptocurrencies that followed, each building on the principles Nakamoto established. From that single white paper, the idea of a decentralized, trustless, and borderless digital currency blossomed into a financial revolution, challenging the dominance of traditional monetary systems and inspiring innovations across industries.

2

Understanding Blockchain Technology

Bitcoin stands as the first and most well-known application of blockchain technology. Originally envisioned as an e-cash transfer system and self-storing currency, Bitcoin quickly evolved into something much larger: a speculative investment asset and the cornerstone of a new financial domain known as cryptocurrencies. The system was designed to incentivize participation through mining, where individuals contributed computational power to validate transactions and secure the network. Miners were rewarded with newly minted Bitcoin for each successfully mined block, creating a mechanism to encourage involvement and ensure the network's sustainability. Furthermore, because the number of Bitcoins generated per block diminishes over time—a process known as halving—this system also introduced a built-in scarcity designed to increase the currency's value as demand grew.

This groundbreaking approach birthed a new field, but it is not without challenges. From technical, economic, and social perspectives, cryptocurrencies and blockchain systems face significant hurdles. For example, the energy-intensive Proof-of-Work consensus mechanism has drawn criticism for its environmental impact. Additionally, advancements in quantum computing pose potential risks to blockchain security, as they could theoretically compromise the cryptographic algorithms that underpin the system. These challenges highlight the urgency for innovation and adaptation to ensure the longevity and feasibility of blockchain technologies.

Blockchain itself is a foundational technology often likened to transformative inventions such as the transistor and the internet. At its core, blockchain enables the secure transfer of digital assets between parties through a decentralized public ledger. Each transaction is ordered sequentially in a chain of cryptographically signed blocks, creating an immutable record. This distributed ledger is accessible to all participants in the network, ensuring transparency and trust, even when the underlying asset is entirely digital, such as cryptocurrencies.

The first complete implementation of a cryptographic blockchain system was Bitcoin, introduced by the pseudonymous Satoshi Nakamoto. Bitcoin enabled the direct transfer of digital assets over the internet without intermediaries, such as banks or financial institutions. This innovative system relies on publicly verified transaction lists, known as blocks, which are cryptographically linked to form a continuous chain. Updates to the ledger occur only when participants reach consensus on a new block, which is then appended to the existing chain.

The implications of blockchain extend far beyond cryptocurrencies. Its potential applications span industries as diverse as supply chain management, healthcare, and governance, offering revolutionary possibilities for secure and transparent data handling. However, the technology's future depends on addressing its current limitations and exploring sustainable alternatives to existing models like Proof-of-Work.

Bitcoin's emergence was a turning point in financial history, introducing blockchain as a transformative force. While challenges persist, this foundational technology continues to inspire innovation and redefine the boundaries of what is possible in a decentralized digital world.

3

Benefits and Risks of Cryptocurrencies

Cryptocurrencies have sparked a global conversation about the future of money. Their advantages—such as privacy, security, and speed—are undeniably appealing, yet these benefits remain largely aspirational in many cases. So, are cryptocurrencies worth the associated costs? The answer depends on the perspective of the user.

For some, particularly organizations or individuals excluded from traditional financial systems, cryptocurrencies have been a lifeline. Lightning-fast peer-to-peer transactions offered by non-Bitcoin cryptocurrencies have proven effective in bypassing financial barriers. For instance, groups like WikiLeaks and other entities cut off from mainstream banking systems have turned to digital currencies as an alternative means of conducting transactions. However, despite these successes, the inherent risks of cryptocurrencies remain. Peg losses, reputational damage, and market volatility underscore the precarious nature of these currencies. Yet with risk comes opportunity, and the digital currency experiment continues to evolve, promising both lessons and innovations.

One of the greatest challenges in evaluating cryptocurrencies is weighing their costs. These costs depend on a range of unpredictable future variables, such as how many people adopt them and for what purposes. For example, Bitcoin's slow transaction speeds, energy-intensive mining process, and high transaction fees make it an impractical choice for everyday purchases—like buying a cup of coffee. The environmental impact of Bitcoin's Proof-of-Work system is another critical concern, as widespread adoption would require significant changes to energy consumption patterns, potentially conflicting with global climate goals.

If the demand for cryptocurrencies skyrocketed, drastic measures might be required to sustain their operation. Options could include incentivizing miners with substantial monetary rewards—essentially creating a system that mirrors the inefficiencies of printing and distributing physical currency. Alternatively, platforms could introduce unrelated rewards to facilitate coin generation. However, this approach would hinge on the continued perception of cryptocurrencies as valuable assets, despite the financial burdens imposed on users through high transaction fees. This uncertainty is a key factor complicating the valuation of digital currencies.

Cryptocurrencies sit at the intersection of opportunity and risk. While they offer solutions to pressing financial challenges, they also raise complex questions about sustainability, scalability, and accessibility. As the digital currency landscape continues to shift, its success will likely depend on innovations that address these critical issues. The ongoing experiment with cryptocurrencies is far from over, and its outcomes will shape the future of finance for generations to come.

4

Cryptocurrency Trading and Investment Strategies

The cryptocurrency market is a dynamic and often volatile space, attracting a diverse range of participants—from casual investors to high-frequency traders. In this chapter, we delve into trading strategies and market behavior, building on foundational discussions of market microstructure.

Investors in the cryptocurrency market often employ different strategies based on their goals and market conditions. High-frequency traders frequently respond to positive momentum, executing numerous trades in rapid succession to capitalize on short-term price movements. Conversely, a smaller subset of investors—sometimes referred to as market makers—engage in longer-term strategies. These participants place high-value orders and hold their assets during periods of negative price momentum, anticipating future gains. This duality in trading behavior illustrates the complex dynamics of the cryptocurrency marketplace.

One theoretical framework sheds light on these patterns. A sorting argument, originally proposed in economic models, explains the asymmetric behavior observed among cryptocurrency traders. In markets dominated by high-frequency investors, price movements often display unique characteristics. For instance, speculative bubbles—a phenomenon where prices rise gradually over time, peak dramatically, and then crash precipitously—are more common in cryptocurrencies than in traditional asset classes such as stocks or foreign exchange. This price formation process reflects the speculative nature of many cryptocurrency investments.

Beyond the trading strategies and behaviors of investors, the cryptocurrency ecosystem is shaped by a variety of human actors, including miners, developers, and users. However, traders and investors represent the majority, contributing significantly to market activity. Price histories in the cryptocurrency market often reveal unique patterns that set it apart from traditional financial instruments. For example, speculative bubbles and distribution shifts lead to peak prices followed by rapid declines. In contrast, trading volumes in many traditional financial instruments tend to align more closely with their price trends, exhibiting a more symmetric response during price drops.

The distinct behaviors of cryptocurrency markets pose both challenges and opportunities for investors. On one hand, the high volatility and susceptibility to speculative bubbles require careful risk management. On the other hand, these characteristics create opportunities for those who can anticipate market movements or leverage innovative trading strategies. As the cryptocurrency market continues to evolve, understanding these dynamics will be crucial for both new and seasoned investors navigating this ever-changing landscape.

5

Regulatory Challenges in the Cryptocurrency Market

The emergence of virtual currencies has introduced a new frontier in financial law and regulation. As cryptocurrencies continue to gain prominence, governments and institutions worldwide face the challenge of navigating this evolving landscape. Some international and regional bodies have coordinated efforts to address regulatory concerns surrounding the development and use of virtual currencies. However, approaches vary widely across countries.

In certain jurisdictions, cryptocurrencies are subject to the same regulatory frameworks as traditional financial institutions. This includes adhering to stringent rules on anti-money laundering (AML) and combating the financing of terrorism (CFT). Conversely, other nations have outright prohibited the use of virtual currencies, citing concerns about security, fraud, and market volatility. Still, others have adopted a more permissive stance, allowing the use of cryptocurrencies while grappling with how to regulate them effectively. Despite these efforts, cryptocurrency often eludes clear categorization within existing regulatory frameworks, presenting significant challenges for oversight and enforcement.

Developing comprehensive regulatory definitions for cryptocurrencies is a delicate balancing act. Regulators must manage the financial risks associated with digital currencies, such as fraud, money laundering, and market manipulation, while fostering innovation and dynamism in this rapidly advancing field. Overly restrictive regulations could stifle progress, while insufficient oversight might leave the market vulnerable to exploitation.

Cryptocurrencies are a significant milestone in the evolution of digital money and electronic payments. They offer considerable potential to transform financial systems by reducing costs, shortening transaction times, and expanding access to financial services. This is particularly impactful in regions with underdeveloped banking infrastructures, where cryptocurrency platforms could serve as a bridge to financial inclusion. Furthermore, by lowering the costs of cross-border transactions, cryptocurrencies could revolutionize international trade and remittances.

The decentralized, anonymous, and entirely digital nature of cryptocurrencies places them at the forefront of the ongoing digital revolution. Yet, these same features also introduce risks that necessitate thoughtful and adaptive regulatory strategies. For instance, the anonymity associated with cryptocurrencies can be exploited for illegal activities, while their price volatility poses challenges for both individual investors and the broader financial system.

Striking the right regulatory balance is critical to ensuring that cryptocurrencies can thrive as a legitimate part of the global economy. This requires policymakers to remain vigilant and flexible, adapting regulations as the technology and market continue to evolve. A careful approach will enable cryptocurrencies to drive innovation and inclusion while safeguarding against financial and systemic risks.

6

Cryptocurrency and Financial Inclusion

From its inception, the decentralized nature of cryptocurrencies was heralded as a solution to financial exclusion—a way to provide financial services to populations traditionally overlooked by conventional banking systems. In theory, anyone with a mobile phone and internet access could use cryptocurrencies to engage in secure financial transactions without requiring access to a bank. For individuals living in remote or rural areas with limited banking infrastructure, this represented a groundbreaking opportunity. By 2020, it was predicted that global smartphone ownership would surpass five billion, and internet penetration had already reached 52.4%, suggesting the potential for widespread adoption of digital financial tools. However, despite these advancements, the promise of cryptocurrencies as a remedy for financial exclusion has not been fully realized.

Did you know that as many as 1.7 billion adults worldwide still lack access to a bank account? This staggering figure underscores the ongoing challenge of financial inclusion. Even more strikingly, over five billion people remain without access to formal financial services such as loans, savings accounts, or credit cards. Those with access to savings and credit often face significant hurdles, including high inflation rates—averaging 10% annually in some cases—and the burden of fees associated with major bank cards. For many, securing a loan is an arduous, costly process, often restricted to micro, small, and medium enterprises. Furthermore, a significant portion of the population is excluded from traditional financial systems due to the lack of formal identification required to open a bank account.

Trust in the financial system is another significant barrier. Approximately 1.2 billion people cite distrust in formal banking institutions as the primary reason for remaining unbanked. Meanwhile, 1.4 billion individuals rely on informal financial services, such as loans from neighbors or community-based trustees. These informal systems often lack the security and reliability of formal banking, leaving individuals vulnerable to financial instability.

The existing banking infrastructure has also proven inadequate in addressing the needs of the poor and unbanked populations, particularly those in remote and underserved areas. Many banks prioritize clients with high creditworthiness and substantial cash flow, effectively excluding those in need of basic financial services. This "cherry-picking" approach leaves a significant portion of the population without access to essential tools for financial stability and growth.

While cryptocurrencies offer a potential pathway to overcoming these challenges, their adoption as a widespread solution for financial inclusion remains an ongoing experiment. For the promise of digital currencies to be fully realized, significant efforts must be made to address barriers such as internet access, technological literacy, and the volatility of cryptocurrency markets. Only then can these innovative financial systems fulfill their mission of empowering the unbanked and underbanked communities around the world.

7

Cryptocurrency's Impact on Traditional Banking

The traditional banking system evokes images of grandeur and permanence—vaulted ceilings, polished marble floors, and the echo of hushed conversations in dimly lit halls. These institutions have long symbolized stability, control, and authority over the world's financial flows. However, the emergence of cryptocurrencies has sparked a revolution that challenges these age-old bastions of finance.

In a curious anecdote, a friend and I once stood in a bank, marveling at its architecture while collecting stacks of hundred-dollar bills. Each bundle bore anti-burglary paper strips, evidence of the precision with which cash is managed within these walls. Yet, upon examining our account printouts, we realized the withdrawals hadn't originated from the bank itself. Instead, they were traced to automated teller machines (ATMs) scattered across the city—an early sign of how financial transactions were increasingly decentralized, even within traditional banking structures. This moment underscored the tension between the immutability of established banking institutions and the disruptive potential of emerging technologies like cryptocurrencies.

In the summer of 2019, Finn Brunton reflected on this shift in an article for *Computers, Freedom, and Privacy*, a non-profit, non-partisan tech policy publication. With the release of Bitcoin a decade prior, he wrote, "we may have reached up and pulled a secret universe, previously pressed up against our world in every detail, down and among ourselves." This moment marked the beginning of a profound transformation—a "world-historical experiment" that redefined the relationship between digital money and official finance. Brunton characterized the journey of cryptocurrencies as a long and perplexing revolution, offering insights through six carefully crafted acts that illuminated this ongoing tale.

Cryptocurrencies have fundamentally altered the traditional banking narrative, challenging its core principles of centralized authority and institutional control. Decentralized digital currencies, such as Bitcoin, operate on peer-to-peer networks powered by blockchain technology. They eliminate the need for intermediaries like banks, enabling individuals to transact directly and securely. This democratization of finance undermines the traditional banking model, which relies on centralization to maintain control over transactions, savings, and lending.

Moreover, cryptocurrencies introduce a level of transparency and accessibility that traditional banks often struggle to provide. Blockchain technology records every transaction in an immutable public ledger, fostering trust and accountability. In contrast, the opacity of banking operations has occasionally fueled mistrust among consumers, particularly in the wake of financial crises.

However, this revolution is not without its challenges. The volatility of cryptocurrencies, combined with their association with speculative bubbles and potential misuse in illicit activities, has drawn criticism from regulators and traditional financial institutions alike. Banks are now grappling with how to adapt to a world

| 19 | - CRYPTOCURRENCY'S IMPACT ON TRADITIONAL BANKING

where digital currencies coexist with—or potentially supplant—traditional financial systems. Some institutions are exploring blockchain technology to improve efficiency and reduce costs, while others remain wary of the disruptive potential it represents.

The impact of cryptocurrencies on traditional banking is a story still being written. It is a narrative of transformation, tension, and opportunity, as the financial world navigates the coexistence of old paradigms and new possibilities. As Brunton suggests, to understand this evolving landscape, we must continue to gather "tales from it," exploring the implications of this digital revolution and its far-reaching consequences.

8

The Future of Cryptocurrencies

The promise of cryptocurrencies lies in their inherent decentralization—free from the control, issuance, or manipulation of central authorities. Unlike traditional currencies, which can be subjected to inflationary policies and politically motivated management, digital money operates outside the influence of authoritarian regimes and centralized systems. This independence offers an unprecedented opportunity to support the harmonious development of individuals and societies, particularly in regions where free markets remain uneven and prosperity elusive. Cryptocurrencies have the potential to become a transformative force in modern economies, revitalizing the principles of sound money management that were once a cornerstone of global finance, long before the era of unbacked paper money.

As societies grapple with the implications of digital currencies, we can only look to the past and present to glean insights and imagine possible futures. Lionel Robbins, in his 1932 treatise on economics, described the discipline as "the science which studies human behavior as a relationship between ends and scarce means, which have alternative uses." This perspective is especially pertinent when considering the role of blockchain technology and cryptocurrencies in reshaping human behavior and resource allocation. Blockchain is more than just a mechanism for payment; it is the foundational technology behind a growing array of cryptographic digital currencies, which are often referred to as digital cash, digital gold, or simply cryptocurrency.

The evolving landscape of digital money is marked by diversity and rapid innovation. Cryptocurrencies encompass a wide range of initiatives, each tailored to address specific use cases or solve unique challenges. From peer-to-peer transactions to decentralized finance (DeFi) platforms, these technologies demonstrate the potential to bypass traditional financial intermediaries, reduce transaction costs, and increase accessibility. Blockchain itself, as a distributed and immutable ledger, facilitates the seamless exchange and integration of information patterns, driving technological evolution across industries.

The impact of cryptocurrencies extends far beyond finance. Their decentralized nature and technological versatility offer solutions to complex global challenges, including financial inclusion, cross-border remittances, and even the democratization of data ownership. However, achieving these goals requires careful navigation of regulatory landscapes, societal adoption, and technological scalability. The journey of cryptocurrencies remains a grand experiment, one that continues to unfold as new applications and innovations emerge.

The future of cryptocurrencies will be shaped by how societies embrace their potential while addressing their challenges. As digital money evolves, it may redefine our understanding of value, trust, and governance, paving the way for a more interconnected and equitable global economy. The transformative possibilities of this technology remain boundless, with the next chapters of its story still waiting to be written.

9

Case Studies: Cryptocurrency Success Stories

The stories of people amassing wealth from Bitcoin are not merely speculative—they are real and serve as compelling examples of the transformative potential of cryptocurrencies. Since its inception in 2009, Bitcoin has redefined the way we think about money and investment. In its earliest years, Bitcoin could be mined profitably with nothing more than a home computer, and a handful of visionary venture capitalists seized the opportunity to invest in this nascent digital currency. Their foresight allowed them to grow their earnings well before the broader public began to recognize Bitcoin's value and utility.

One of the most famous early anecdotes in cryptocurrency history involves Laszlo Hanyecz, who, in 2010, became the first person to complete a Bitcoin transaction. Hanyecz famously paid 10,000 BTC for two pizzas—a casual exchange at the time but a historic milestone in hindsight. At the time of writing, that sum would be worth approximately $30 million, a staggering demonstration of how far Bitcoin has come since those early days. This transaction highlights the profound and often unpredictable trajectory of cryptocurrencies, especially as they gained traction during a period when many were still recovering from the 2009 global recession.

CASE STUDIES: CRYPTOCURRENCY SUCCESS STORIES

The cryptocurrency market has continued to generate headlines about extraordinary returns. Initial Coin Offerings (ICOs) raising $60 million in just 30 minutes and early investors reaping returns of up to 2,000% are tantalizing examples that fuel the perception of endless opportunities to build fortunes in this space. However, while the potential for wealth creation is undeniable, it is equally important to recognize the inherent risks associated with these assets. Cryptocurrencies remain a volatile and highly speculative investment, and caution must always accompany optimism.

For the majority of people—especially those who do not engage in full-time trading—cryptocurrencies represent more than just a path to quick profits. They signify a fundamental shift in how we perceive and interact with money. Beyond financial speculation, digital currencies offer a personalized means of exchange, a way to securely store wealth, and a platform for leveraging transformative technology.

The success stories surrounding cryptocurrencies provide valuable lessons about the opportunities and challenges of this revolutionary market. While tales of wealth can captivate and inspire, they should also remind us to approach this evolving landscape with both enthusiasm and prudence. As the cryptocurrency experiment continues to unfold, its impact on individuals and economies alike will undoubtedly remain a source of fascination and innovation.

10

Cryptocurrency and Cybersecurity

Cryptocurrencies like Bitcoin are often depicted as both a technological marvel and a double-edged sword. While they represent a groundbreaking financial innovation, their decentralized and pseudonymous nature has also raised concerns about misuse by malicious actors. These digital currencies are alleged to provide criminals with an unregulated financial vehicle, offering a means to escape detection, access extortion payouts around the clock, and transfer illicit income across borders almost instantaneously. By exploiting hard-to-track currency swaps, such actors can launder gains and evade traditional financial oversight mechanisms. The result is a new challenge for cybersecurity experts and regulators alike.

Cybercriminals deploy a variety of methods to exploit digital systems, often targeting individuals, businesses, and institutions. Attacks may occur on a small scale, infecting a single computer, or involve widespread schemes such as phishing campaigns and spam attacks. Malicious software—ranging from viruses to ransomware—remains a primary tool in the arsenal of attackers. These viruses, often sold in bulk, are constantly evolving, with attackers trading code and tools to outpace existing defense measures. The cybersecurity community is in a perpetual race against so-called "hero antiviruses," solutions designed to neutralize the latest wave of attacks.

The widespread potential for cryptocurrency misuse underscores the unresolved relationship between the average user and digital money. Despite Bitcoin's status as a public digital ledger—an open book in theory—it has become synonymous in public discourse with criminal acts and hacking. This association is particularly unfortunate because, in practice, cryptocurrencies are often less prone to misuse than conventional fiat instruments like virtual gift cards or prepaid vouchers, which remain popular tools for illicit activities.

Beyond enabling criminal acts, cryptocurrencies have also become entangled in cybercrime through ransomware attacks. In these cases, attackers use malicious software to lock a user's files, demanding payment—often in cryptocurrency—in exchange for unlocking them. In more covert instances, compromised computers are silently co-opted into mining cryptocurrencies for attackers, generating illicit income in the background without the user's knowledge.

The decentralized and digital nature of cryptocurrencies poses unique challenges for cybersecurity. It blurs traditional lines of accountability and jurisdiction, complicating enforcement and prevention efforts. However, it also offers an opportunity to rethink and improve digital security systems.

While cryptocurrencies are not inherently to blame for cybercrime, their growing adoption has highlighted the importance of robust cybersecurity measures. As digital money evolves, so too must our defenses, ensuring that these innovations can thrive safely and responsibly in an increasingly interconnected world.

11

Cryptocurrency and Money Laundering

Long before the advent of digital currencies, even as far back as the late 19th century, visionaries like Alexander Graham Bell recognized the inefficiencies of traditional banking systems. Bell considered developing a system where people could send and receive cash electronically, much like sending a letter through a postal service. This idea, revolutionary for its time, envisioned a world where financial transactions bypassed banks entirely. However, technological limitations of the era forced Bell to abandon this pursuit. His vision, while ahead of its time, serves as a reminder that people have long sought alternatives to conventional banking systems.

Throughout history, anonymous methods of transferring funds—such as wire transfers—have provided opportunities for dishonest individuals to conceal and move illicit gains. With the emergence of cryptocurrencies, this concept has been reimagined. Digital money offers a new frontier for financial transactions, but its decentralization, pseudonymity, and global accessibility make it particularly appealing to those engaged in illegal activities. Cryptocurrencies provide criminals with the means to remain anonymous, access extortion payments at any time, and quickly transfer funds across borders. These activities bypass traditional banking oversight and complicate efforts to trace the origin and destination of illicit wealth.

One of the most significant concerns related to the misuse of cryptocurrencies is money laundering. The decentralized nature of digital currencies makes them an attractive tool for obscuring the source of illicit funds. Criminals can exploit cryptocurrency technologies to facilitate a range of illegal activities, from drug trafficking to organized crime financing. By moving assets through multiple hard-to-track currency swaps and decentralized exchanges, they can effectively "clean" their money, making it appear legitimate.

The technology underpinning cryptocurrencies is central to their use in money laundering schemes. Blockchain, while transparent and immutable, also provides opportunities for obfuscation. Techniques such as mixing services (also known as tumblers) and privacy-focused cryptocurrencies like Monero or Zcash can anonymize transactions, making it difficult for authorities to trace illicit activities. These features, while innovative, pose significant challenges to law enforcement and financial regulators tasked with combating money laundering.

Addressing these challenges requires a thoughtful and proactive approach to regulation. Many countries have begun implementing measures to mitigate the risks posed by cryptocurrencies. These include Know Your Customer (KYC) and Anti-Money Laundering (AML) requirements for cryptocurrency exchanges, as well as efforts to improve international cooperation in tracking illicit transactions. However, the effectiveness of these measures hinges on balancing the need for oversight with the preservation of innovation and privacy.

The relationship between digital currencies and money laundering highlights the dual-edged nature of technological advancement. While cryptocurrencies have the potential to revolutionize global finance and increase financial inclusion, they also require robust frameworks to prevent misuse. By fostering collaboration between governments, financial institutions, and technology developers, we can work toward a future where digital currencies are both secure and transparent.

12

Cryptocurrency and Taxation

The taxation of cryptocurrency has emerged as a critical and complex issue, reflecting the challenges posed by rapidly evolving technologies. The pace of cryptocurrency innovation has often outstripped the ability of regulatory bodies like the Internal Revenue Service (IRS) and Congress to address fundamental legal and policy questions. Without amendments to existing tax laws, it remains difficult for the IRS to apply the Internal Revenue Code (IRC) to these emerging digital assets. This gap has created legal ambiguity and uncertainty regarding the proper tax treatment for taxpayers involved in cryptocurrency transactions.

Under current guidance, the IRS categorizes cryptocurrencies as property rather than currency. This classification means that transactions involving cryptocurrencies are subject to capital gains and ordinary income tax laws. For example, if a taxpayer uses cryptocurrency to purchase goods or services or exchanges it for another digital asset, they are required to report any gains or losses based on the asset's market value at the time of the transaction. However, many areas remain unclear, such as how to tax staking rewards, airdrops, and transactions involving privacy-focused cryptocurrencies. Further guidance is essential to address these ambiguities and provide clarity for taxpayers.

In March 2018, the IRS Criminal Investigation Division introduced the Virtual Currency Compliance Initiative to address compliance issues among cryptocurrency users. This program seeks to identify cryptocurrency account holders and wallet addresses that fail to comply with U.S. tax laws. As part of its enforcement efforts, the IRS has also issued subpoenas to cryptocurrency exchanges to obtain information about users, underscoring its commitment to ensuring tax compliance in the digital currency space. Subsequent IRS updates have provided additional guidance on the tax treatment of cryptocurrencies, but more comprehensive regulations are needed to keep pace with the rapid evolution of blockchain technologies.

When discussing cryptocurrency taxation, it is essential to have a clear definition. According to the IRS, cryptocurrency—also referred to as virtual or digital currency—is a decentralized digital asset that relies on encryption for security and operates independently of any central authority. Bitcoin, Ripple, and Ethereum are among the most popular cryptocurrencies today. Since the introduction of Bitcoin in 2009, the cryptocurrency market has experienced exponential growth, with a combined market capitalization exceeding $900 billion. Daily transaction values in recent years have hovered around $150 billion, reflecting the widespread adoption and integration of digital currencies into the global financial system.

As blockchain technology and cryptocurrency markets continue to evolve, the need for a modernized tax framework becomes increasingly apparent. Effective regulation must strike a balance between fostering innovation and ensuring compliance. Policymakers will need to address emerging complexities, such as cross-border transactions, decentralized finance (DeFi) platforms, and the use of privacy-enhancing technologies. By providing clearer guidance and adapting tax policies to this rapidly changing landscape, regulatory bodies can help cryptocurrency achieve its potential while maintaining transparency and fairness.

13

Cryptocurrency and International Remittances

The world of international remittances is poised for transformation, and cryptocurrencies are at the forefront of this evolution. Traditional money-transfer services are often costly, slow, and cumbersome, making them an imperfect solution for millions of people relying on cross-border payments. Cryptocurrencies, by contrast, offer a faster and more affordable alternative, particularly as adoption grows.

Consider the case of a hypothetical user who chooses Tether (a stablecoin pegged to the US dollar) to send remittances. The process is remarkably straightforward: she opens an account with a supported cryptocurrency exchange, converts US dollars into Tether, and then inputs the recipient's wallet address on the platform. In an instant, the recipient receives the funds and can convert the Tether into local currency. While the process does incur some transaction costs, these fees are significantly lower than those charged by traditional money-transfer companies. For individuals with a solid cryptocurrency background, further savings can be achieved by carefully adjusting buy and sell orders in decentralized marketplaces.

Blockchain technology, which underpins cryptocurrencies, also reduces transaction costs when converting digital currencies into other forms of money. This innovation is a game-changer in the remittance space, offering substantial benefits to both senders and recipients. However, the full potential of cryptocurrencies in this arena has been constrained by regulatory hurdles.

International remittances are vital for many economies, yet they remain expensive, difficult to trace, and susceptible to regulatory barriers. Cryptocurrencies have the potential to address these challenges, streamlining the process of sending money across borders without relying on traditional financial networks. However, efforts to meet anti-money laundering (AML) and counter-terrorism financing (CTF) regulations often complicate the process. The bureaucratic burden of verifying remittance transactions can inadvertently hinder legitimate transfers while remaining ill-equipped to detect actual illegal activity.

Despite these obstacles, cryptocurrencies are beginning to disrupt the remittance industry. Although only a small fraction of global remittances currently use cryptocurrencies, the ripple effects are undeniable. Digital currencies enable faster, cheaper, and more efficient transfers, making them a compelling alternative to established financial institutions. As blockchain technology and regulatory frameworks continue to mature, the use of cryptocurrencies for remittances is likely to expand.

The promise of cryptocurrencies in the remittance space lies in their ability to empower underserved populations. By lowering costs and increasing accessibility, they have the potential to bridge gaps in the global financial system, particularly for individuals in remote or economically disadvantaged regions. However, unlocking this potential will require overcoming regulatory challenges and fostering greater trust and adoption.

Cryptocurrencies are already showing glimpses of their transformative power in international remittances. As the industry evolves, these digital currencies may play a central role in shaping a more inclusive and efficient global financial ecosystem.

14

Cryptocurrency and Decentralized Finance (DeFi)

Decentralized Finance, or DeFi, is a transformative concept that exemplifies the broader objectives of Web 3.0. At its core, Web 3.0 envisions a peer-to-peer, decentralized network that redistributes power from centralized corporations to individual users, creating a more equitable and balanced digital ecosystem. Within this vision, DeFi stands out as one of the most impactful innovations, offering financial services traditionally monopolized by institutions such as banks, stock markets, and insurance companies. Through blockchain technology, DeFi has made it possible to replicate and even surpass these services on a decentralized, transparent, and accessible platform.

Despite its potential, many people question why anyone would choose to bypass traditional financial institutions. However, those deeply embedded in cryptocurrency communities often share a common sentiment of distrust toward centralized financial systems. This disillusionment stems from several reasons:

1. **Lack of Transparency**: Centralized institutions operate with limited transparency, leading to distrust among individuals who demand greater accountability.

2. **Exclusion and Inequality**: Traditional banks often marginalize individuals without high creditworthiness or sufficient collateral, leaving large portions of the population underserved.
3. **Centralized Control**: The concentration of power in traditional financial systems creates vulnerabilities, including susceptibility to corruption, mismanagement, and restrictive policies.
4. **High Costs**: Fees and charges associated with traditional financial services can be prohibitive, particularly in cross-border transactions and lending.
5. **Limited Accessibility**: Centralized systems often fail to serve individuals in remote or economically disadvantaged regions, leaving them without essential financial services.

DeFi offers a revolutionary alternative to these centralized structures by leveraging the power of blockchain technology. This decentralized model enables individuals to participate directly in financial activities such as lending, borrowing, trading, and investing, without relying on intermediaries. Smart contracts—self-executing agreements coded onto the blockchain—ensure transparency, efficiency, and trust, replacing the need for human intermediaries.

The idea that "the revolution won't be centralized" is gaining traction across various sectors, including finance, technology, and governance. Traditional financial institutions have historically acted as gatekeepers, controlling transactions, assets, and access to financial opportunities. In contrast, DeFi represents a shift toward a more inclusive and heterogeneous network, built on principles of openness, collaboration, and decentralization.

The broader implications of DeFi extend beyond finance. If the renewed vision for the internet—characterized by sharing, decentralization, and user empowerment—is to become a reality, blockchain technology will play a pivotal role. By shifting power from intermediaries to end-users and producers, blockchain lays the foundation for a truly decentralized digital economy.

As DeFi continues to evolve, it challenges traditional notions of finance, creating opportunities for innovation and inclusion. While there are still hurdles to overcome, including regulatory uncertainty and technological scalability, the potential of DeFi to reshape global financial systems is undeniable. It stands as a critical step toward the decentralized future envisioned by Web 3.0.

Conclusion

The rise of cryptocurrencies has undeniably captured the imagination of investors and technologists worldwide. While their appeal lies in their decentralized nature and the technological innovation they represent, it is important to remind potential investors to also consider traditional investment methods for long-term financial stability. The widespread enthusiasm for digital currencies is often rooted in dissatisfaction with the responses of traditional financial markets to economic uncertainties and geopolitical challenges. These frustrations have driven efforts to enhance transparency and mitigate systemic risks within financial markets—a pursuit that must also extend to the rapidly expanding world of digital assets.

Despite the excitement surrounding cryptocurrencies, their adoption for mainstream economic transactions remains limited. It is unlikely that digital currencies will replace traditional means of exchange in the near future. However, the interest sparked by these alternative stores of value has already begun to deliver significant technological advancements that address real-world challenges. From improving cross-border transactions to creating new financial solutions, the ripple effects of cryptocurrency innovations are reshaping the technological landscape.

Perhaps the most profound impact of cryptocurrencies will be felt within the financial sector itself. Cryptocurrencies have challenged the very foundations of financial intermediation by enabling households and non-financial institutions to perform critical roles traditionally handled by banks. These roles include credit analysis, risk assessment, and liquidity provision, all of which are now made possible through peer-to-peer networks. This shift diminishes the reliance on centralized financial institutions, redistributing power and providing users with greater control over their financial assets.

As the cryptocurrency experiment continues to unfold, it serves as a catalyst for reimagining the future of finance. The development of decentralized financial systems has the potential to increase accessibility, reduce costs, and empower individuals worldwide. However, realizing this potential requires a balanced approach—one that supports innovation while ensuring stability and transparency in the global financial ecosystem.

Cryptocurrencies may not yet be the dominant medium for economic exchange, but their impact is undeniable. They have inspired a wave of technological progress that will continue to shape the financial sector and society at large, leaving a legacy that extends far beyond their initial promise.

Enjoyed This Book? Let Others Know!

If this book has blessed, encouraged, or challenged you in any way, I'd love to hear about it! Your review not only helps others discover this message but also encourages me to keep writing.

Would you take a moment to share your thoughts? A few sentences on what stood out to you can make a big difference.

You can leave a review on Amazon, Goodreads, or wherever you purchased this book. Thank you for being part of this journey!

www.ingramcontent.com/pod-product-compliance
Lightning Source LLC
LaVergne TN
LVHW092101060526
838201LV00047B/1507